The Whale in the Well

Written by Maureen Haselhurst
Illustrated by Andrew Selby

Long ago, a whale was trapped in a well.
Years passed and she forgot all about the world outside.

One day, there was a noise and a little frog tumbled down into the well.

“Goodness,” giggled the frog,
“you look gloomy!
Come and see
the wonderful new world
outside.”

The frog pushed and pulled
but he could not move the whale.
How the whale wished she could
see the wonderful new world.

High on the mountain top,
the Storm Bird pounded
its powerful wings
and the ground shook.
A great shower of rain fell.

The rain washed the whale out of the well.

"Goodness, look at those cliffs!" said the whale.

"It's a town," giggled the frog.

“A sea monster!” said the whale.
“It’s a ship,” said the frog.

"A rainbow!" said the whale.
"It's a bridge," said the frog.

"There's so much to see!"
said the whale.

So the whale and the frog
set off to see
the wonderful new world.